Cheshire Verses
Edited by Heather Killingray

First published in Great Britain in 2007 by:
Young Writers
Remus House
Coltsfoot Drive
Peterborough
PE2 9JX
Telephone: 01733 890066
Website: www.youngwriters.co.uk

All Rights Reserved

© Copyright Contributors 2006

SB ISBN 978-1 84602 769 7

Foreword

Young Writers was established in 1991 and has been passionately devoted to the promotion of reading and writing in children and young adults ever since. The quest continues today. Young Writers remains as committed to the nurturing of poetic and literary talent as ever.

This year's Young Writers competition has proven as vibrant and dynamic as ever and we are delighted to present a showcase of the best poetry from across the UK and in some cases overseas. Each poem has been selected from a wealth of *A Pocketful Of Rhyme* entries before ultimately being published in this, our fourteenth primary school poetry series.

Once again, we have been supremely impressed by the overall quality of the entries we have received. The imagination, energy and creativity which has gone into each young writer's entry made choosing the poems a challenging and often difficult but ultimately hugely rewarding task - the general high standard of the work submitted ensured this opportunity to bring their poetry to a larger appreciative audience.

We sincerely hope you are pleased with this final collection and that you will enjoy *A Pocketful Of Rhyme Cheshire Verses* for many years to come.

Contents

Arden Primary School
Hannah Shenton (10)	1
Jake Atkinson (9)	2
Charlotte Watson (9)	3
Victoria Cope (9)	4
Ben Wallace (9)	5
Cara Woodward (8)	6
Matila Dunning	7
Abigail Haworth (9)	8
Callum Hatton (8)	9
Amy Gage	10
Hannah Littlewood (7)	11

Bollington St John's CE (Aided) Primary School
Joseph Stubbs (9)	12
John Cunniffe (9)	13
Sophie Marshall (11)	14
James Greensmith (10)	15
Daniel Mayers (10)	16
Sarah Wallace (9)	17
Charlotte Harrison (9)	18
Liam Hinkley (9)	19
Craig Dentith (10)	20
Brandon Davies (9)	21
Adam Thomas (11)	22
Clare Greenhalgh (10)	23
Edward Cox (9)	24
Mollie Ledgar (9)	25
Oliver Kershaw (10)	26
Jack Daley (9)	27
Curtis Hyde (10)	28

Capenhurst CE Primary School
Cameron Weaver (7)	29
Henry Cornes (7)	30
Dion Pover (8)	31
Elston Kavanagh (7)	32
Aidan Carroll (8)	33

Rachel Evans (8)	34
Mustafa Elsherkisi (8)	35
Darragh Ward (7)	36
Holly Cousins (7)	37
Emma Jaynes (7)	38
Samuel Robertson (7)	39
Samantha Griffin (8)	40
George Chong (7)	41
Sophie Davis (7)	42
Josh Weston (9)	43
Alexandra Jones (9)	44
Chloe Howling (8)	45
Radha Evans (10)	46
Oliver Knight (10)	47
Harry McElhinney (9)	48
Poppy Murphy (9)	49
Chloe Lodge (9)	50
Joe Jaynes (9)	51
Aboudi Elsherkisi (9)	52
Jack Wilson (9)	53
Evelyne Duncan (10)	54
James Warrington (10)	55
Charlie Parker (10)	56
Jonathan Holt (9)	57
Elliot Goodwin (9)	58
Jack Keenan (9)	59
Charlotte Evans (10)	60
Charlotte Robinson (10)	61
Thomas Cornes (10)	62
Georgia Lamb (10)	63
Clinton Lee (9)	64
Shaun Luke Wiggins (9)	65

Crowton Christ CE Primary School

Laura Bielinski (10)	66
Katy McKeown (10)	67
Rebecca Annells (9)	68

St Ambrose RC Primary School, Stockport

Danielle Hope (10)	69
Alysha Webber (11)	70

Ashleigh Kennerk (10) — 71
Jamie Morris (9) — 72
Callum Cahill (9) — 73
Dominic Chase (9) — 74
Paddy Maguire (9) — 75
Marc Wakefield (8) — 76
Jordan Moores (9) — 77
Cynthia Lau (8) — 78
Abigail Jackson (10) — 79
Zoe Billington (10) — 80
Adam Bircher (9) — 81
Daniel Keeble (10) — 82

St Chad's CE Primary School, Winsford
Caitland Walton (8) — 83
Bradley Woodward (8) — 84
Jack Grant (8) — 85
Thomas Taylor (9) — 86
Melissa Leigh (9) — 87
Amy Hassall (9) — 88
Charlie Kirk (8) — 89
Kayleigh Mitchell (8) — 90
Megan Lewis (8) — 91
Lee Bennett (8) — 92
Ricky Wallis (8) — 93
Bridey Stevens (8) — 94
Casey Washburn (8) — 95

St Luke's CE School, Warrington
Donna Harrison (9) — 96
Daniel Horton (9) — 97
Julia Roberts (10) — 98
Myles Duffy (9) — 99
Thomas Jones (9) — 100
Elliott Harvey (9) — 101
Jack Baines (9) — 102
Caitlin Dutton (9) — 103
Chloe Murphy (9) — 104
Jessica Singleton (9) — 105
Rachel Gaskell (9) — 106
Eleanor Bradford (9) — 107

Hollie Moore (10) 108
Josch Fairhurst (9) 109
Arran Heaton (9) 110
Charlie Hewitt (10) 111

St Raphael's RC Primary School, Stalybridge
Bethany Shelmerdine (10) 112
Liam Fullard (11) 113
Rhys Hadfield (10) 114
Jack Fieldhouse (10) 115
Michael Mansfield (10) 116
James Shields (10) 117
Simon Kenworthy (10) 118
Jack Forrest (10) 119
Chelsea Coop (10) 120
Emma Cunningham (10) 121
Matthew Wardle (10) 122
Joshua Ormerod (10) 123
Robert Holding (11) 124
Liam Manley (10) 125

Whitby Heath Primary School
Hayley Sparks (9) 126
Cerys Holleron (8) 127
Daniel Arathoon (9) 128
Robyn Mercer (8) 129
Jordan Shrewsbury-Gee (9) 130
Emily Rigby (9) 131
Amy Hammond (7) 132
Siobhan Franka (8) 133
Callum Hayes (9) 134
Hannah McMurray (9) 135
Olivia Garland (8) 136
Lauren Spruce (9) 137
Nevielle Hearfield (9) 138
Tyler (10) 139
Jake Ranley (9) 140
Katie Gooding (9) 141
Morgan Basnett (9) 142
Lauren Evans (7) 143
Helen Lyth (10) 144

Eleanor Wightman (8)	145
Christopher Anderson (11)	146
Leah Woods (9)	147
Emily McCubbing (9)	148
Jessica Swindells (7)	149

Wistaston Junior School

Alice Simons (10)	150
Grace Newton (10)	151
Liam Smyth (10)	152
Louis Cain (10)	153
Kyle Nicholas (10)	154
Felicity Martin (10)	155
Jack Bohannan (10)	156
Jack Steele (10)	157
Adam Elson (10)	158
Alex Heaton (10)	159
Joshua Banks (10)	160
Casey Ramsden (10)	161
Konnor Edge (10)	162
Sam Hough (10)	163
Ruairidh Johnstone (10)	164
Alexander Flude (10)	165
Thomas Slaney (8)	166
Molly Ramsden (9)	167
Selina O'Neill (9)	168
Oliver Slaney (8)	169
Bryce Bennett (8)	170
George Rowlands (8)	171
James Hartshorn (8)	172
Emma Hassall (8)	173
Natasha Adams (8)	174
David Palmer (8)	175
Lucy Brierley (8)	176
Oliver Parker (8)	177
Tia Redmond (8)	178
Rebecca Davies (8)	179
Bryony Chapman (10)	180
Hannah Davies (11)	181
Hannah Thompson (10)	182
Sam Spencer (10)	183

Callum Parker (10)	184
Sarah Oakley (10)	185
Rhys Bennett (10)	186
Tom Corbett (10)	187
Charlotte Curry (10)	188
Harry Robinson (10)	189
Joanne Freake (10)	190
Ellis Lawley (10)	191
James Burgess (11)	192
Stephanie Walkington (10)	193
Rebecca Jones (10)	194
Josh Golding (11)	195
Lauren Reece (10)	196
Jenna Shephard (11)	197
Abbie Broadgate (11)	198
Alexander Fitton (10)	199
Alice Woodbridge (10)	200
Alan Hoodless (11)	201

The Poems

Animals Are All Different

Cheetahs are my favourite animals you know,
So are dogs, so are cats,
So are rabbits, so are snakes,
So are kangaroos, so are spiders,
Oh no! not spiders, don't like them.

Hannah Shenton (10)
Arden Primary School

What The Romans Ate For Tea

I never knew what a Roman ate for his tea;
But then a Roman came to me and said . . .
Well, first comes tasty rabbit stew
And then the stuffed dormouse
Next we have the buttered snails
And this is how it goes
We will have juicy beef
With the wine we made
I eat with my family
And with all my friends
I thanked the Roman for his time
For telling me what he ate.

Jake Atkinson (9)
Arden Primary School

A Pet

'Mum everyone's got a pet at school,
Can I have a dragon?'
'Don't be a fool!'

'Why don't you have a hamster instead?'
'Nah I prefer an anteater,
With a big fat head.'

'Well can I have a dog with a tail?'
'As long as you feed it,
Without fail.'

'Or can I have a kangaroo,
There's one for sale at the zoo?'
'No you cannot, our garden's tidy,
Have you forgot?'

'Well can I have a snake?'
'No, but I'll buy you a fake,'
'But I want something that's alive,
That will eat the bees in the hive.'

'Come on let's go out before I shout,
No you'll like where we're going.'
'What getting a lawnmower for the mowing!'

But when we arrived at the shop
I jumped, I shouted, I leapt, I hopped,
Then when we got back to the house,
I realised my pet, a baby mouse.

Charlotte Watson (9)
Arden Primary School

Sunbed

Man,
I bet you a tenner I could get a tan,
On a sunbed as hot as a frying pan.
I will cram myself in there as fast as I can
It could be first it could be last.
It could be slow it could be fast.
It could be the future it could be the past.

Victoria Cope (9)
Arden Primary School

The Dragon Competition

I couldn't throw it in the bin.
I just wanted to win.
Should I go to the dragon land,
Or should I stay in my heavy metal band?
I had decided what I was going to do.
I was going to see the dragon
Dragoon!
But before I set off to this wondrous place
I had to tie my big, long lace.

Ben Wallace (9)
Arden Primary School

Unicorns

They twinkle like stars
They are as white as snow
They have manes like horses
Their feet clip clop like high-heeled shoes
Their horns twinkle with multicoloured sparkles
The fairies flutter all around them and they are as magic as anything.

Cara Woodward (8)
Arden Primary School

Untitled

I know this boy at school that thinks he knows it all,
But when he tries to think his head sounds like a tap
Dripping in an empty sink drip, drop,
The boy who finds it hard to think.

Matila Dunning
Arden Primary School

What Next?

Read a story,
Watch TV,
Chase my cat,
Or climb a tree?

It's quite good fun,
To grow some cress,
But most of all,
Let's make a mess!

Paint the walls,
Spill the glue,
Sprinkle glitter,
All over you!
Wear your very oldest dress,
Then,
Make a marvellous
Mixed up muddlesome,
Bound to get,
Into troublesome,
Splashing, spluttering,
Rub-dub-dubblesome,
Spotted, stripy,
Rainbow coloursome,
Mega, multi
Mountainous
Mess!

Abigail Haworth (9)
Arden Primary School

Goodnight

Goodnight,
Sleep tight,
Wake up bright,
In the morning light
To do what's right
With all your might.

Callum Hatton (8)
Arden Primary School

Rainbow

The colours of the rainbow,
I'll share with you,
Red, yellow, indigo and green,
Orange, violet and blue
Rainbows are beautiful
Rainbows are bright
Rainbows are seen
But not at night.

Amy Gage
Arden Primary School

The Fairy Times Table

1am casting spells,
2am ringing bells,
3am danger trials in every way,
4am flying high over the sky,
5am dancing lessons,
6am wishes granted,
7am OK, children fly, flutter or walk home.

Hannah Littlewood (7)
Arden Primary School

Football

Man Utd are good, Villa are bad
Cheer here, cheer there, another cheer for Man Utd there.

Man Utd are good, Arsenal are bad
You should support Man Utd Dad.

Man Utd are good, Everton are bad
You should support Man Utd lad.

Man Utd are good, Liverpool are bad
Jack you should support Man Utd lad.

Joseph Stubbs (9)
Bollington St John's CE (Aided) Primary School

Seasons

Summer, spring, winter, autumn, it's all so much for me
Hot, falling leaves, growing trees, cold, it's all so much for me
It's all so much for me.

Cold, winter, sun, summer, growing trees, autumn,
Spring flowers, it's all so much for me,
It's all so much for me.
I like summer, winter, autumn, spring, so much,
It's so confusing.

John Cunniffe (9)
Bollington St John's CE (Aided) Primary School

Colours

Red are roses,
Green are trees,
White are doves,
Yellow are bees.

I like swimming,
Just like you,
My favourite colour,
Is light blue.

I like colours,
Especially blue,
Every single one,
And so do you!

Sophie Marshall (11)
Bollington St John's CE (Aided) Primary School

I Can See The Sea!

Can you see what I can see?
I can see the deep blue sea.

Can you see the old mighty blue whale,
Swimming along and thrashing its tail?

Can you see the swishy seaweed
Swirling about where the fish feed?

Can you see the sailing boat
Whizzing about fast and slow?

Can you see the cruiser ship
Chugging around like a frying chip?

Can you see what I can see?
I can see the deep blue sea!

James Greensmith (10)
Bollington St John's CE (Aided) Primary School

World War II

Planes fly high in the dark night sky
Bombs dropping and lots of people die.

The big and noisy tanks
Digging up the grassy banks.

All the soldiers carry big guns
Fathers, husbands, brothers and sons.

All the children were sent away
Somewhere safe for them to stay.

Daniel Mayers (10)
Bollington St John's CE (Aided) Primary School

I Wish I Was A Bird

I wish I was a bird,
Then I could fly away,
Leave all my troubles behind,
Then I could find a way,
To cope with life on Earth.

If I was a bird,
I would have such fun,
Swooping in the sky,
My feathers warm in the sun,
It would be such fun.

Sarah Wallace (9)
Bollington St John's CE (Aided) Primary School

How Different!

A bookshop without books
A model without looks
A summer without sun
A child without fun,
A last name without a first
A bonfire without a colour burst,
A winter without snow,
A deer without a doe,
How strange would the world be like that?
No animals, dogs or cats,
No birds, no bees, no bats!

Charlotte Harrison (9)
Bollington St John's CE (Aided) Primary School

Football Mad

I'm football mad
I'm football mad.
If City win I'll be glad
But if they don't I'll be sad.

At the great Wembley up north
Standing to the south they all come forth.
As City beat the mighty United
Everybody else is so excited.

Liam Hinkley (9)
Bollington St John's CE (Aided) Primary School

My Pets

My goldfish swam around the bowl
In the filter there is a hole
Flipper my goldfish finds a stone
Flipper will always love his home
Kipper my second goldfish swims about
Then I heard a terrible shout
It was my mum running about
My favourite programme was on
But I couldn't watch it
Because there the sun shone.

Craig Dentith (10)
Bollington St John's CE (Aided) Primary School

The Fly

The fly is annoying and disturbing.
It is the great fly of the dead.
It likes the taste of bread.
When I'm reading my book I get fed.
It sleeps on my bed.
It is not very dead.
It has health.

Brandon Davies (9)
Bollington St John's CE (Aided) Primary School

Chocolate

I love chocolate,
Do you too?
It's great, it's tasty, you can even get it made to look like you!

You can buy chocolate in a bar,
But instead of a bar,
My mum has got a chocolate car!

Adam Thomas (11)
Bollington St John's CE (Aided) Primary School

The Moon

The moon is a great big tomb
It sits on top of a loom
One day soon
It might go *boom!*

With no moon way up high
No more darkness across the sky
More light shining, oh why?
The sun will be blazing and we would sigh.

With sun all the time, it would be hard to sleep
The rivers and lakes wouldn't be so deep
All the plants would start to weep
And fall down without a peep.

The fields would not be so neat
The cows would give less meat
Food would be a treat
Thirst would be the one to beat.

If suddenly the moon came back
The Earth would get back on track
Lots of fruit and vegetables to pack
Off to the supermarket in a big sack.

Thank goodness for the light and the dark
They both make their mark
The sun can shine with a spark
The moon cast its shadow over the park.

Clare Greenhalgh (10)
Bollington St John's CE (Aided) Primary School

Sports

Football is fantastic,
Ping-pong is ballistic,
Tennis is tough,
Rugby is rough,
Badminton is tense,
And hockey is lots of pence.

Edward Cox (9)
Bollington St John's CE (Aided) Primary School

Dolphins In The Air

Dolphins, dolphins, jumping in the air
Swimming around going nowhere
Jumping out and in like
A bouncy bear going somewhere.

Dolphins, dolphins, swimming fast
On the way to save a friend
Dolphins everywhere
Playing around with a teddy bear
Dolphins, dolphins, jumping in the air.

Mollie Ledgar (9)
Bollington St John's CE (Aided) Primary School

I Have Got A . . .

I have got a freaky cat, who wears
A party hat!

I have got a fat dog, which eats lots
Of hot dogs!

I have got a cute little rabbit, which
Eats lots of Weetabix!

I have got a goldfish, I eat it on my
Dish!

I have got a parrot, which eats lots
Of carrots!

Oliver Kershaw (10)
Bollington St John's CE (Aided) Primary School

Sports

At six foot seven and seven foot eight,
Basketball players are usually great,
They reach up high they reach up tall,
None of the basketball players are very small.

Football players train very hard,
In the match they hope they don't get shown a card.
Penalty shoot-out miss or score,
If you hit the back of the net you'll hear the crowd roar.

Athletics events are really fun,
I especially like the 100 metre run.
Gold medals, silver medals too!
All the athletes hope they'll win a few!

Golf players play a lot,
They all hope they'll swing the perfect shot.
Hit it with a golf club onto the green,
Hit it so high it can't be seen.

Jack Daley (9)
Bollington St John's CE (Aided) Primary School

Football Boots

I walk onto the football pitch,
With my brand new boots,
But at half-time
They were a muddy crime.

At the end of the match,
I ordered another batch,
Gold, silver and even thatch,
Brand new boots for a new match.

Curtis Hyde (10)
Bollington St John's CE (Aided) Primary School

Dinosaur

Quiet sleeper
Fast runner
Pouncing jumper
Jumping higher
Fighting harder
Meat eater.

Cameron Weaver (7)
Capenhurst CE Primary School

Ghosts And Skeletons

I think skeletons are very weird
Because they can't grow a beard.

They don't have any skin
Unfortunately they're always thin.

Ghosts are sometimes scary
I wonder if they are ever hairy.

If I met a skeleton or a ghost I would say,
'Everybody be quiet today.'

Henry Cornes (7)
Capenhurst CE Primary School

Emma The Dinosaur

Emma the dinosaur was so thin
So I took her to my school,
So she ate her meal and the dinner ladies,
Then she had a swim in the sea,
And she met a dinosaur called Jessica.

Dion Pover (8)
Capenhurst CE Primary School

My Bad Dinosaur

My T-rex is very naughty
Because he eats my doughnuts
And he tries to eat my horse.
But I catch him doing it.
My pet dinosaur eats the TV set
And he killed my aunty Bet
That was cold and wet.
He ate the fridge
He's very naughty.

Then he was forty.
He had a party
And the dinosaur was called Barty.
He nearly blew up my house,
Then he ate my pet mouse.

He was one
Then my T-rex got a bomb
And he chased my friend Tom
Then he went to Dick and Dom
He was so naughty
I just could not cope
So I gave him to another bloke.

Elston Kavanagh (7)
Capenhurst CE Primary School

Stegosaurus

My pet stegosaurus
He lives in my house
He has a nouse
Then there was a fast mouse
He destroyed our school.

Aidan Carroll (8)
Capenhurst CE Primary School

My Dinosaur Pet

If I wanted to touch the moon
It would be no problem
I could just ask my dinosaur
To give me a lift
Other people will have to take a rocket
Make sure you remember to lock it
Sometimes he is a bad dinosaur pet
One time he ate the TV set
He is sometimes very bad,
But I think it would be easier if I didn't have a lad.
So I got a girl dinosaur
She was midge and even she
Ate the fridge.

Rachel Evans (8)
Capenhurst CE Primary School

My T-Rex

My pet dino is a T-rex
She is so very naughty
One day she ate the TV set
Then eventually the next day
I caught her in a net.

Mustafa Elsherkisi (8)
Capenhurst CE Primary School

Lunchtime Play

Crunch goes my lunch.
Shout out and make lots of noise!
Everyone *yell* at the bell.
The sun helps make the fun.
The girl twirls and makes herself *dizzy*.
The boy has a toy called *Buzz Lightyear*
The ball is kicked up in the tree so tall,
The bell rings and *stops* it all.

Darragh Ward (7)
Capenhurst CE Primary School

When I Started School

When I started school everything was different
There was a lot of children.
There was none like me
I found my class at last.
What animal are you?
Are you Mrs Crew?
Why I am a
Pteranodon.

Holly Cousins (7)
Capenhurst CE Primary School

Dinosaurs Can

Dinosaurs can roar roar
Dinosaurs can eat people
They can crunch
Dinosaurs can have babies
Dinosaurs can bathe themselves
Dinosaurs can charge
Dinosaurs can get killed.

Emma Jaynes (7)
Capenhurst CE Primary School

My Pet T-Rex

My pet T-rex is very naughty
Because he ate the fridge
Then I got a Smallosaurus
And he was midge
And he didn't eat the fridge.

Then the Smallosaurus ate my T-rex
Which was not a problem really
Because the T-rex
Was very, very naughty.

Samuel Robertson (7)
Capenhurst CE Primary School

Dinosaurs

Earth wrecker
People killer
Suspicious murder
Blood licker
Big eater
Flesh eater
Bone crusher.

Samantha Griffin (8)
Capenhurst CE Primary School

My Dinosaur Friend

One day there was a dinosaur who came for tea.
Because he was my friend who can do a lot of bends.
Quite a friend he is.
But sometimes he lends my games
My friend is nice but insane
Climbs planes.
And he's good at telling jokes
But then he got a croak
In his voice
So he can't tell jokes anymore.
Then he got his voice back, so he can tell jokes
And someone fell for one of the jokes.

George Chong (7)
Capenhurst CE Primary School

Ted The Tyrannosaurus

Ted the tyrannosaurus rex went to Tyrannosaurus town fair.
He entered the big, shaggy game for dinos with big hair.
He also entered the park race
He ran quite fast, until he was red in the face
And as you all know he came in last place.

Sophie Davis (7)
Capenhurst CE Primary School

My Teacher Thinks . . .

My teacher thinks I'm measuring angles but actually . . .
I'm swimming in beans with sausages falling on me
I'm bouncing on marshmallows with chocolate sauces
I'm soaring through potato skin with cheese on top.

My teacher thinks I'm reading but really . . .
I'm surfing with dolphins in the Mediterranean Sea
I'm skating with penguins on ice in Antarctica
I'm climbing on branches with chimpanzees.

My teacher thinks I'm writing a story but actually . . .
I'm acting with James Bond otherwise known as 007
I'm working out on the football pitch and I am getting cheered on.
I'm touching down for an American football team.

My teacher thinks I'm researching 'rivers' but really . . .
I'm boxing with Tyson in America
I'm playing football with Steven Gerrard for England
I'm recording 'Top of the Pops' reloaded show with Sam and Mark.

My teacher thinks I am working hard but little does she know . . .

Josh Weston (9)
Capenhurst CE Primary School

My Teacher Thinks . . .

My teacher thinks I'm measuring angles but actually . . .
I'm swimming in a pool full of melted ice cream
I'm ice skating on a slippery lolly ice
I'm diving in a pool of frothy hot chocolate.

My teacher thinks I'm reading but actually . . .
I'm teaching a cheetah to do gymnastics
I'm chasing an antelope from Madagascar
I'm swimming with bright blue dolphins flipping 100 metres high.

My teacher thinks I'm writing a story but little does she know . . .
I'm shopping in space with Nelly Furtardo
I'm having dinner at Steve Gerrard's house
I'm dancing with Rhianna in her studio.

My teacher thinks I'm researching 'rivers' but actually . . .
I'm getting my medal because I've beaten Colin Jackson
I'm getting the cup as I've won the FA football
I'm receiving my cheerleading kit as I've completed my gymnastics
My teacher thinks I've worked hard but little does she know . . .

Alexandra Jones (9)
Capenhurst CE Primary School

Dinosaurs

Bone cruncher
Meat eater
Dinosaur meater
Evil killer
Fish smeller
Predator spotter
Leaf eater
Bad killer
Dragonfly spotter
Dinosaurs.

Chloe Howling (8)
Capenhurst CE Primary School

My Teacher Thinks . . .

My teacher thinks I'm measuring angles but actually . . .
I'm swimming through melted chocolate and multicoloured
Sprinklers drifting down on my head.
I'm having tea on a dolphin's back.
I'm skating through vegetable soup.

My teacher thinks I'm reading but really . . .
I'm having a ride on a tiger's back in the long green grass.
I'm going somersaults with a monkey in the trees.
I'm drifting down the ocean on a whale's tummy.

My teacher thinks I'm writing a story but actually . . .
I'm dancing with Girls Aloud in a pop DVD
I'm chatting with Mary Kate and Ashley in London.
I'm singing with Shayne Ward in New York.

My teacher thinks I'm researching 'rivers' but really . . .
I'm on a trampoline with Britney Spears.
I'm on a horse with the Pussycat Dolls in Spain on the beach.
I'm playing hockey with Robbie Williams.

My teacher thinks I'm working hard but little does she know . . .

Radha Evans (10)
Capenhurst CE Primary School

My Teacher Thinks . . .

My teacher thinks I'm measuring angles but actually . . .

I'm sliding through a banana split
I'm an ice-cube turning, swirling, sliding in glass of orange juice
I'm canoeing through gravy.

My teacher thinks I'm reading but I'm actually . . .

I'm sliding down a dolphin's back into the sea
I'm bouncing on an elephant's back
I'm hopping over crocodiles through the swamp.

My teacher thinks I'm writing a story but actually . . .

I'm listening to Basil Brush jokes
I'm experimenting with Sooty, Sweep and Sue
I'm racing against Ant and Dec on 'Beat the Bugs'

My teacher thinks I'm researching 'rivers' but really . . .
I'm in a tournament against Tim Henman
I'm starting a race with Kelly Holmes
I'm in athletics with greyhounds.

Oliver Knight (10)
Capenhurst CE Primary School

What My Teacher Thinks . . .

My teacher thinks I'm measuring angles but actually . . .
I'm eating through a banana with cream.
I'm ice skating on humbug
I'm dancing with chips in a bowl.

My teacher thinks I'm reading but really . . .
I'm jumping off an elephant's back
I'm racing against a cheetah in a zoo
I'm skateboarding on giraffes in the jungle.

My teacher thinks I'm writing a story but actually . . .
I'm playing football with Mikel Arteta
I'm on a mission with James Bond underwater
I'm singing with Robbie Williams in Asia.

My teacher thinks I'm researching 'rivers' but actually . . .
I've just won a football match 5-2
I'm running 150 metres with Kelly Holmes in the Olympics.
I'm playing rugby with Johnny Wilkinson in Brazil.

My teacher thinks I'm working hard but little does she know . . .

Harry McElhinney (9)
Capenhurst CE Primary School

My Teacher Thinks . . .

My teacher thinks I'm measuring angles but I'm . . .
Being chased by Haribo bears.
I'm swimming in a gravy-filled Yorkshire pudding.
I'm surrounded in beautiful amber-orange seeds.

My teacher thinks I'm reading but really . . .
I'm having a shower under an elephant.
I'm doing gymnastics with an orang-utan
I'm cuddling up to a cheetah cub under the sun.

My teacher thinks I'm writing a story but actually . . .
I'm laughing my head off with Harry Hill's jokes
I'm on safari with Nigel Marvin stalking a T-rex.
I'm bloated with Jamie Oliver's food.

My teacher thinks I'm researching 'rivers' but . . .
I'm cheerleading with the warriors.
I'm searching for some trainers for Beckham.
I'm gobsmacked at Kelly Holmes' time for the cross country.

My teacher thinks I am working hard but little does she know . . .

Poppy Murphy (9)
Capenhurst CE Primary School

My Teacher Thinks . . .

My teacher thinks I'm measuring angles but actually . . .
I'm playing netball in a bowl of hot chocolate.
I'm swimming in a bowl of vanilla ice cream, with baby sprinkles all over.
I'm dancing in a pool of spaghetti.

My teacher thinks I'm reading but really . . .
I'm riding on a back of a rhino raging through the desert.
I'm racing a cheetah through the back legs of an elephant.
I'm trying to catch an eagle flying to its nest.

My teacher thinks I'm writing a story but actually . . .
I'm riding the jiggy bank with Ant and Dec on Saturday Night Takeaway.
I'm dancing with Robbie Williams in the Queen's palace.
I'm singing with Britney Spears in a farm.

My teacher thinks I'm researching 'rivers' but really . . .
I'm playing football against England.
I'm swimming with the top swimmers.
I'm doing gymnastics with Kelly Holmes.

My teacher thinks I am working hard but little does she know . . .

Chloe Lodge (9)
Capenhurst CE Primary School

My Teacher Thinks . . .

My teacher thinks I'm measuring angles but actually . . .
I'm skiing down a hill of tomato ketchup,
I'm sunbathing on the largest chip buttie,
I'm rock climbing up a fish.

My teacher thinks I'm reading but actually . . .
I'm riding on the back of the largest blue whale,
I'm racing on the back of a tiger,
I'm competing in a jumping contest against a kangaroo.

My teacher thinks I'm writing a story but actually . . .
I'm racing a car with Fernando Alonso,
I'm interviewing Elvis Presley
I'm playing football at Anfield with Steven Gerrard.

My teacher thinks I'm researching 'rivers' but really . . .
I'm winning the Wimbledon cup,
I'm playing cricket against Australia,
I'm playing golf against Colin Montgomery.

Joe Jaynes (9)
Capenhurst CE Primary School

My Teacher Thinks . . .

My teacher thinks I'm measuring angles but actually . . .
I'm jumping through Cheerios with chocolate milk.
I'm sleeping on soft marshmallows with ice cream.
I'm bouncing on a pizza with pepperoni.

My teacher thinks I'm reading but really . . .
I'm chasing a cheetah with blue spots.
I'm swimming with the slimy crocodiles.
I'm bouncing on a kangaroo's back.

My teacher thinks I'm writing a story but actually . . .
I'm racing with Michael Schumacher
I'm playing football with Steven Gerrard
I'm singing with Chicco.

My teacher thinks I'm researching 'rivers' but really . . .
I'm playing tennis and I'm winning two more points
I'm in a running race and won gold
I'm playing golf and got a 'hole in one'.

My teacher thinks I've worked very hard but little does she know . . .

Aboudi Elsherkisi (9)
Capenhurst CE Primary School

My Teacher Thinks . . .

My teacher thinks I'm measuring angles but actually . . .
I'm rafting on chips in vinegar.
I'm hitching a ride on gummy worm's back.
I'm climbing up a Turkish Delight mountain.

My teacher thinks I'm reading but . . .
I'm counting the stripes on a tiger's back.
I'm dancing with a chimpanzee.
I'm on the trampoline with an elephant.

My teacher thinks I'm writing a story but actually . . .
I'm dribbling with Ronaldo.
I'm saving a goal with Robinson.
I'm on the jiggy bank with Ant and Dec.

My teacher thinks I'm researching 'rivers' but really . . .
I'm scoring a goal for Manchester United
I'm playing baseball with The Simpsons
I'm hitting the ball in a cricket match.

My teacher thinks I'm working hard but little does she know . . .

Jack Wilson (9)
Capenhurst CE Primary School

My Teacher Thinks . . .

My teacher thinks I'm measuring angles but actually . . .
I'm roller skating on dark chocolate.
I'm doing backflips on vegetable lasagne.
I'm doing cartwheels on chicken korma.

My teacher thinks I'm reading but really . . .
I'm riding on the back of a Siberian tiger.
I'm on safari, racing against a lion.
I'm going back in time, seeing the dinosaurs.

My teacher thinks I'm writing a story but actually . . .
I'm playing my electric guitar with McFly.
I'm chatting to Harry Potter on the four dragons.
I'm in the Tardis with David Tennant.

My teacher thinks I'm researching 'rivers' but really . . .
I'm racing on the racing track with Kelly Holmes.
I'm at Wimbledon with Andrew Murray.
I'm on the cricket pitch with the England team.

My teacher thinks I'm working hard but little does she know . . .

Evelyne Duncan (10)
Capenhurst CE Primary School

MY Teacher Thinks . . .

My teacher thinks I'm measuring angles but actually . . .
I'm swimming in a pool of melted chocolate
I am bouncing on a planet of marshmallows
I am running around the world on a potato.

My teacher thinks I'm reading but really . . .
I'm riding a rhino on a racetrack
I'm chasing a red cheetah around the globe
I'm doing gymnastics with a chimpanzee.

My teacher thinks I am writing a story but actually . . .
I'm on a secret mission with James Bond
I'm dancing to Robbie's song as he sings
I'm singing with Shayne Ward.

My teacher thinks I'm researching 'rivers' but really . . .
I'm running in the Olympics and going to win the gold
I'm playing with Tiger Woods and I won the PGA sport 2006
I'm playing football and my fans are cheering me on.

My teacher thinks I'm working hard but little does she know . . .

James Warrington (10)
Capenhurst CE Primary School

My Teacher Thinks . . .

My teacher thinks I'm measuring angles but actually . . .
I'm canoeing on a freezing strawberry ice lolly.
I'm swimming in a pool of hot fudge.
I'm bouncing on a trampoline of stretchy chewing gum.
I'm climbing a tree of green broccoli.

My teacher thinks I'm reading a book but actually . . .
I'm being bounced by elephants' big white tusks.
I'm swimming in a swamp of slimy crocodiles.
I'm sleeping in the nests of some colourful parrots.
I'm kick-boxing against a massive kangaroo.

My teacher thinks I'm writing a story but actually . . .
I'm playing football in the Tipton with Zack and Cody.
I'm practising basketball with Zac Efron.
I'm on an adventure with Peter, Susan, Edmund and Lucy.
I'm teasing Lizzie with Matt McGuire.

My teacher thinks I'm researching 'rivers' but really . . .
I have won the Golf Open against Tiger Woods.
I'm playing football with Steven Gerrard.
I'm thrashing Tim Henman in a game of tennis.
I've beat Mr Bruce in a guitar contest.

My teacher thinks I've worked hard but little does she know . . .

Charlie Parker (10)
Capenhurst CE Primary School

My Teacher Thinks

My teacher thinks I'm measuring angles but actually . . .
I'm slurping grapefruit on grapefruit island,
I'm jet-skiing through strawberry milkshake,
I'm rock climbing up a stick of sticky rock.

My teacher thinks I'm reading but really . . .
I'm kick-boxing against a kangaroo,
I'm dive-bombing with two metre penguins,
I'm headbutting rhinos in a gigantic cave.

My teacher thinks I'm writing a story but actually . . .
I'm presenting the gold award to Shayne Ward,
I'm co-piloting Michael Schumacher in a yellow Mini,
I'm throwing apple pies at Megan with Drake and Josh.

My teacher thinks I'm researching 'rivers' but really . . .
I'm golfing on top of the Milky Way,
I'm playing tennis in Asia,
I'm swimming across the Atlantic Ocean.

My teacher thinks I'm working hard but little does she know . . .

Jonathan Holt (9)
Capenhurst CE Primary School

My Teacher Thinks . . .

My teacher thinks I'm measuring angles but actually . . .
I'm swimming through a pool of chocolate milkshake,
I'm eating grapes in Rome in the Emperor's Palace,
I'm rock climbing up a cliff of candy canes.

My teacher thinks I'm reading but really . . .
I'm playing battle-tag with an angry rhino,
I'm kick boxing with a scary kangaroo,
I'm water-skiing with geckas in the Great Barrier Reef.

My teacher thinks I'm writing a story but actually . . .
I went to Boston and played with Zack and Cody,
I'm shopping with London Tipton,
And I'm dancing with Max and Tapeworm.

My teacher thinks I'm researching 'rivers' but really . . .
I'm playing against Matt McGuire in Wimbledon
I'm having a game of Baseball with Raven and Cory Baxter,
And I'm surfing with Bart Simpson.

My teacher thinks I'm working hard but little does she know . . .

Elliot Goodwin (9)
Capenhurst CE Primary School

My Teacher Thinks . . .

My teacher thinks I am measuring angles but actually . . .

I am sinking in a bowl of ice cream covered in colourful sprinkles.
I am sliding through a banana split.
I am swimming in a bowl of gravy.

My teacher thinks I am reading but really . . .

I am swimming in shark infested waters.
I am boxing with a bold kangaroo.
I am jumping from crocodile to crocodile.

My teacher thinks I am writing a story but actually . . .

I am dancing on Chicco's video.
I am telling jokes with Peter Kay.
I am skateboarding with Tony Hawks.

My teacher thinks I am researching 'rivers' but really . . .

I am a professional football player and I have just scored a goal.
I am running 400 metre hurdles with Kelly Holmes.
I am playing tennis with Tim Henman.

My teacher thinks I am working really hard but little does she know…

Jack Keenan (9)
Capenhurst CE Primary School

My Teacher Thinks . . .

My teacher thinks I'm measuring angles but actually . . .

I'm skating on an orange 'FAB' ice cream
I'm daydreaming on a beach made out of chocolate
I'm swimming in a bowl of wine gums.

My teacher thinks I'm reading but really . . .
I'm doing cartwheels on top of an elephant
I'm lying on top of a chocolate horse
I'm learning to talk in dog language.

My teacher thinks I'm writing a story but actually . . .
I'm dancing with Rachel Stevens in her new album
I'm singing with Kelly Clarkson in New York
I'm singing karaoke with Avril Lavigne in Spain.

My teacher thinks I'm researching 'rivers' but really . . .
I'm horse riding through a chocolate mountain
I'm in the Olympics doing high jump
I'm scuba-diving with Georgie.

My teacher thinks I'm working hard but little does she know . . .

Charlotte Evans (10)
Capenhurst CE Primary School

My Teacher Thinks . . .

My teacher thinks I'm measuring angles but actually . . .
I'm climbing up a chocolate mountain
I'm riding up a vanilla ice cream hill with strawberry sauce.
I'm swimming in amongst the jam of a doughnut.

My teacher thinks I'm reading a book but actually . . .
I'm chasing a lion through a cave.
I'm twisting and driving with a giraffe.
I'm swimming underwater with a whale.

My teacher thinks I'm writing a story but actually . . .
I'm singing at a concert on the beach at new Brighton with the Pussycat Dolls
I'm running in a race with Shayne Ward
I'm swimming with Robbie Williams in his pool in California.

My teacher thinks I'm researching 'rivers' but really . . .
I'm in the Olympics throwing a javelin.
I'm doing long jump with Jonathan Edwards
I'm playing in a rugby match with the England team.

My teacher thinks I'm working hard but little does she know . . .

Charlotte Robinson (10)
Capenhurst CE Primary School

My Teacher Thinks . . .

My teacher thinks I'm measuring angles but actually . . .
I'm swimming in a bowl of thick chocolate.
I'm snowboarding on a strawberry ice cream hill
I'm swimming in a bowl of squished fruit.

My teacher thinks I'm reading but really . . .
I'm racing against a raging rhino
I'm on the back of a chocolate Labrador
I'm on the back of a big, bad tiger.

My teacher thinks I'm writing a story but actually . . .
I'm doing a secret mission with James Bond.
I'm dancing with Elton John.
I'm in a Ferrari with Richard Hammond.

My teacher thinks I'm researching 'rivers' but actually . . .
I'm racing on a motor cross on a wet muddy field.
I'm racing a Formula 1 car against Michael Schumacher.
I'm playing for England against Brazil.

My teacher thinks I'm working hard but little does she know . . .

Thomas Cornes (10)
Capenhurst CE Primary School

My Teacher Thinks . . .

My teacher thinks I'm measuring angles but actually . . .
I'm drowning in a bowl of spaghetti and they're strangling me
Getting tighter and tighter,
I'm bouncing on a plate of pink and white marshmallows,
I'm diving off a dark chocolate diving board and plunging into
The warm pool of melted chocolate.

My teacher thinks I'm reading a book but really . . .
I'm dancing with a graceful flamingo with its wings flapping,
I'm sliding down an elephant's trunk over and over again,
I'm swinging with a monkey through the deep forest.

My teacher thinks I'm writing a story but actually ., . .
I'm shooting goals at Paul Robinson and running around the pitch
                                              when it goes in,
I'm on a mission with James Bond under the sea,
I'm running with Paul Crone and waving as I go.

My teacher thinks I'm researching 'rivers' but really . . .
I'm running in the Olympics against Kelly Holmes
I'm playing golf with Tiger Woods,
I'm throwing the ball into the net, beating Australia 13-0.

My teacher thinks I'm working but little does she know . . .

Georgia Lamb (10)
Capenhurst CE Primary School

My Teacher Thinks . . .

My teacher thinks I'm measuring angles but actually . . .
I'm flying on a frisbee pizza.
I'm fighting with a portion of chips.
I'm eating a ham sandwich on the River Thames.

My teacher thinks I'm reading but really . . .
I'm riding on a donkey and jumping over hills.
I'm flying on an eagle soaring over the skies.
I'm giving a pig a piggyback.

My teacher thinks I'm writing a story, actually . . .
I'm shooting a scene with James Bond.
I'm doing the X-Factor with Simon Cowell.
I'm meeting Sam and Mark at TMI.

My teacher thinks I'm researching 'rivers' really . . .
I'm scoring the World Cup goal.
I'm racing against Schumacher.
I'm playing against Andy Murray at Wimbledon.

My teacher thinks I'm working but little does she know . . .

Clinton Lee (9)
Capenhurst CE Primary School

My Teacher Thinks . . .

My teacher thinks I'm measuring angles but actually . . .
I'm diving into a massive pile of pizza with pepperoni on it
I'm swimming in a big bowl of ice cream with sprinkles on the top
I'm sliding down a chocolate covered ice cream.

My teacher thinks I'm reading but actually . . .
I'm riding wild on the back of a rhino rampaging into everything
I'm doing the limbo underneath a giraffe
I'm sitting under a cheetah sleeping while dreaming about eating
                                                                   loads of food.

My teacher thinks I'm writing a story but actually . . .
I'm secret agent 007 Bond. James Bond
I'm playing football with Wayne Rooney against Brazil
I'm singing in a high school musical with Troy Boulton.

My teacher thinks I'm researching 'rivers' but really . . .
I'm playing football with David Beckham taking free kicks at an
                                                                     open goal
I'm running wild with Kelly Holmes in the Olympics
I'm playing cricket with Freddie Flintoff in the Ashes.

My teacher thinks I'm working hard but little does she know . . .

Shaun Luke Wiggins (9)
Capenhurst CE Primary School

Mysterious Shapes

In the faint evening sun,
Flowing side to side,
Like a pendulum in a wise, old clock,
So tall, so wispy,
The ground is its body,
The breeze is its breath,
It is invisible to touch,
Yet smooth to see.

It never sleeps,
Nor does it eat,
But so alive and dancing in the late September glow,
Its friends are the autumn golden leaves,
Its protection, its power are the twisting trees.

Though as light fades out,
Its dancing ends,
The airy shape disappears behind the clouds
Only to be seen when the sun shines again,
It'll reappear,
It's a shadow.

Laura Bielinski (10)
Crowton Christ CE Primary School

It's Not The Same Anymore

It's not the same since Izzy died,
Carrots are carrots,
Never cantered, never galloped.

It's not the same any more,
No saddling up now,
No going to shows.

It's not the same now,
I can't bring myself to call,
There's no reason to do so.

Her head collar hangs on the garage door,
The lead rope is dusty now,
Never forgetting what I had with my horse,
The way I believed in her,
The way I loved her.

The bucket is empty now,
No food to make,
No water to pour,
That's how my life dropped to the ground.

My new haircut won't be ruined,
By getting eaten,
Now I can paint peacefully,
In the yellow and orange sun,
But it still won't be the same.

It's just not the same any more since Izzy died,
A small part of me died,
All I have is pictures and memories,
Thousands of them.

It's just not the same anymore.

Katy McKeown (10)
Crowton Christ CE Primary School

My Poem About Everything

There's five in the family I live with,
1st Dad, 2nd Mum, 3rd James, 4th Michael and I'm 5th.
I'm the youngest because I'm nine,
But I'm the only girl, so I can keep my brothers in line.
We're not at all small, in fact I'm quite tall,
We all play sport, and I play netball.
We've got a rabbit called Smudge,
And James did have a hamster called Fudge.
My birthday's on February the 3rd,
Which is totally absurd.
I adore school,
I think it's cool.
I'm now in class four,
I really like it, so does everyone else I'm sure.
My brother James, he is great,
Especially in rugby, as he runs straight.
Michael is ace,
And he's like me, because he has freckles all over his face!
I enjoy skipping, it's brilliant fun,
I also love the weather in summer, as it's usually all sun.

Rebecca Annells (9)
Crowton Christ CE Primary School

The Aquarium

Four small crabs,
Crawling across the shore,
Some crab hunters came,
And took one away.

Three adult seahorses racing today,
One was so speedy it flew away,
A fisherman caught him,
And yelled 'Hip hip *hooray!'*

Two dancing dolphins,
Swimming home today,
They were spinning,
Trying to be dizzy.

Now there are
Three small crabs,
Two adult seahorses
One dancing dolphin.

Danielle Hope (10)
St Ambrose RC Primary School, Stockport

Shark's Days

Shark sobbed, scraped
Walls under sea, shuffled
Over from his girlfriend.
Smartly wrote a poem,
Smiled seriously but slowly
And softly.

Alysha Webber (11)
St Ambrose RC Primary School, Stockport

Untitled

W hopping waves just went through the sea
A nd a miniature fish went with it
V ibrating, rippling oceans
E volves into a colossal wave
S ewage staining the tide.

Ashleigh Kennerk (10)
St Ambrose RC Primary School, Stockport

The Cheeky Kangaroo

The hippitty hoppitty kangaroo escaped from the zoo.

It bounced into town causing mischief as he hopped from Shop to shop.

The police got in cars but the kangaroo said, 'How bizarre You can't catch me.'

But . . . they shot the roo in his tracks
With a sleeping dart.

They caged the kangaroo and put it in the zoo
And it never got away again.

Jamie Morris (9)
St Ambrose RC Primary School, Stockport

The Lion

I saw a lion in the zoo.
And it had a big poo.
Why it had a poo I don't know?
I left the zoo.
When I came back it grew.
The lion is roaring.
The lion is big.
The lion is a fat pig.
The lion is eating.
It choked on its food.
So now it's dead.
I went to see the other lions.
Then all the other lions choked on their food too
So now they are dead
So I wish they weren't dead.

Callum Cahill (9)
St Ambrose RC Primary School, Stockport

The Bean Race

And now for the race
The broad bean got stuck in a tunnel
The runner bean won
The jelly bean wobbled
The baked bean ran in heat
The green bean went to Parliament
The string bean went on the rack
The Heinz bean went in a pot.

And the winner is the runner bean for coming first.

Dominic Chase (9)
St Ambrose RC Primary School, Stockport

The BHG

The BHG (Big Horrible Giant)

Waiting in your wardrobe
Till you fall asleep,
He'll pop out and at you
Starting with your feet,
He'll spit out your toenails
And your bogies too,
He'll save them for pudding
Then he'll say 'Blesshu!'
When you wake up and find out that you're dead,
He'll wait in your garden shed . . .
Till you're back in bed.

Paddy Maguire (9)
St Ambrose RC Primary School, Stockport

The Furious Lion

In the jungle the ferocious lion is hunting for food,
The lion waits in the long grass waiting for food to come.
A deer came and the lion charged for the deer.
The deer ran, the lion caught up quick and munched,
Crunched and hunched.
The lion got caught in a massive net and thought maybe
Someone can help.
So he screamed help.

Marc Wakefield (8)
St Ambrose RC Primary School, Stockport

Skeletons

S keletons are scary
K ick butt
E verybody is scared of them
L ie and they will kill you
E arly one night they will come
T hey hate you
O n Christmas they are making a plan
N ever believe.
S keletons are dead.

Jordan Moores (9)
St Ambrose RC Primary School, Stockport

Dolphins

D olphins
O ctopus
L azy shark
P enguin
H ats fell on the sea
I s a fish
N ormal dolphins
S pecial dolphins.

Cynthia Lau (8)
St Ambrose RC Primary School, Stockport

Teachers

T eachers are the best
E nd of fighting and crying
A piece of work that is so hard
C an you find your great big star?
H ere is your bag miss, now you can go to the bar
E ars wide open to start a new lesson
R eams of people begin to dig
S he wants to say, 'Bye Miss, see ya on Monday.'

Abigail Jackson (10)
St Ambrose RC Primary School, Stockport

Dolphins

Dolphins, dolphins swim in the sea up and down
You are big and blue, big thing who swims in the sea
With lots of fish and sharks and lots of other things down there.
I am big so let me swim in the big open sea so go, go leave
 me alone.

Zoe Billington (10)
St Ambrose RC Primary School, Stockport

Caterpillar, Caterpillar

Caterpillar, caterpillar, where art thou caterpillar?
How beautiful you look,
The butterfly you will transform to,
Should be put into a book.

Your elegancy is so exquisite,
Your beauty so divine,
You are so elegantly great,
I want you to be mine.

The cocoon you soon will be in,
That birds cannot get through,
Will be hard to penetrate,
So they cannot kill you.

The beauty you will witness soon,
Is more lovely than pure gold,
It will end so suddenly,
The weather will get cold.

So lay your eggs and fly away,
For fate will cleanse your luck,
The people will see your fine looks,
And put them in a book.

Adam Bircher (9)
St Ambrose RC Primary School, Stockport

When I Went To School

When I went to school,
I was a star but I fell out of the sky
Not because I was dim or thin
Because I was too bright and I gave
Everyone a fright.
I tell you they were dim, not me.
I am a star and I am too bright
And that is why I gave everyone a fright.

Daniel Keeble (10)
St Ambrose RC Primary School, Stockport

Hail

You are strong like a bone
You come down fast from the sky
You are as hard as a baseball
But I don't know why.

I hear a *'pitter-patter'*
A twirl when you hit the ground
Around and round.

You are as hard as the ground
You are as hard as a tree
You are as cold as ice.
You scare me.

Caitland Walton (8)
St Chad's CE Primary School, Winsford

Hurricane

You are very strong
And you spin round and round.
You can suck things high
Off the ground.

You twirl so fast
That I can feel your air
Spinning round and round whipping through my hair.

You made a loud noise twirling around
There were screams when you picked people off the ground.

I opened the door
And I felt really scared
I froze on the spot and stopped and stared.

Bradley Woodward (8)
St Chad's CE Primary School, Winsford

Hurricane

He saw a hurricane
The wind blew his kite
It swirled round and round
Until it was out of sight.

He felt a hurricane
Coming his way
He was in a strange country
That he visited for the day.

He heard a hurricane
As loud as a rock band
Playing in the street
Swirling in the sand.

I feel like crying
In my bed
Beside my mum
As she rubs my head.

Jack Grant (8)
St Chad's CE Primary School, Winsford

Sunny

You are yellow and orange
You are like a sphere
You are very shiny when I look at you
When I wake up you are here.

You feel like a hot oven
Beaming down on me
On my holiday
When I was in the sea.

I hear birds singing
Children having fun
Whenever they see
The shining sun.

I feel really hot
I just want to dive
In a swimming pool
That's how I survive.

Thomas Taylor (9)
St Chad's CE Primary School, Winsford

Snow

When I looked out of the window
The ground was covered in snow
It looked like a blanket
And the sunshine made it glow.

I opened the door and
It felt so smooth
But I don't know why
I could not move.

When I opened my window
People playing in the snow
It looked so exciting
I wanted to go.

I feel quite happy
When it snows
I can make a man
With a carrot nose.

Melissa Leigh (9)
St Chad's CE Primary School, Winsford

Fog

You are black and dark
You make it hard to see
You cannot see a lot
I can't even see me.

You are very strong
You move so slow
You disappear in my hands
You're softer than snow.

When I go out I can hear
Wind blowing all around
I can hear little stones
Dropping on the ground.

You are wonderful to see
But I feel scared and sad
Because it's really dark
I feel very bad.

Amy Hassall (9)
St Chad's CE Primary School, Winsford

Hail

You are very rare
You are very hard
You ripple on the ground
And crunch in my backyard.

You bounce on the ground
Like a bouncy ball
You're like frozen rain
And from the sky you fall.

I hear you
Crunch on the ground
You lash down
It's a horrible sound.

I feel warm inside
When you hail
Like a really warm fire
But you make me pale.

Charlie Kirk (8)
St Chad's CE Primary School, Winsford

Hail

I walked out the door
I saw drops of hail
Falling from the sky
So white and so pale.

It felt very soft
But also very hard
Small balls of ice
Bouncing on my yard.

I heard hail drumming
On the roof
And it sounded like
A horse's hoof.

I feel happy
When hail comes down
It's fun getting wet
But my mum gives me a frown.

Kayleigh Mitchell (8)
St Chad's CE Primary School, Winsford

Sunny

You are as yellow as a banana
Bigger than a bus,
If you look too close
You will make such a fuss.

You are as warm as a water bottle
When I go outside
So I jump in the sea
Then here comes a tide.

I can hear my skin when it starts to peel,
Water drying on the table
So I can eat my meal.

I feel happy
In the sun
I stroke my dogs
And we have lots of fun.

Megan Lewis (8)
St Chad's CE Primary School, Winsford

Snow

I woke up in the morning
I had such a fright
Snow was falling
So we had a snow fight.

It was falling very slowly
From the sky
Like little white clouds
Floating by.

You feel as soggy as jelly
You feel as soft as cakes
You are slow coming down
In your delicate flakes.

I can hear you crunch
When I walk on the floor
I stepped carefully
Stepped out of the door.

When I feel
Feel sad
Cold as an ice-cube
It's very bad.

Lee Bennett (8)
St Chad's CE Primary School, Winsford

Hail

You are as round as a marble
You fall like a speeding car
You are white and shiny like a star.

You are as hard as a brick
You are as cold as ice, you bounce like a ball
You are as little as a mouse.

When I squash you,
You make a crunchy sound.
You tap on the floor when you hit the ground.

You make me feel like Jack Frost
And a little piece of snow
You are very cold, like when the wind blows.

Ricky Wallis (8)
St Chad's CE Primary School, Winsford

Wind

You are very windy
And you are as stormy as a snowball
You are as cold as a fly
And you make things fall.

You are very strong
You can push trees down
You can destroy buildings
When you come to town.

I feel my hair blowing
As the wind goes by
I feel my clothes get wet
As I start to fly.

I hear the wind
As it flies by
There's a fly
Whistling in the sky.

Bridey Stevens (8)
St Chad's CE Primary School, Winsford

Rain

When the sky turns grey
You can feel it's going to rain
For the rest of the day
Oh it's such a pain.

Big drops of water
Start to fall
They splash onto the ground
'Pitter-patter,' they call.

It feels like my hands in the shower
It makes me feel cold
And I shiver like a flower.

I jump up and down
And I touch the ground
And I turn around
When I am in my gown.

Casey Washburn (8)
St Chad's CE Primary School, Winsford

The Greedy Monster

I found a monster in my bed and it said,
'Help, help, I need to be fed.'
So I took it to the kitchen and then I said,
'Monster, monster, do you like white bread,
With cheese and ham or a biscuit instead?
So monster, monster do you like white bread?'
The monster replied, 'I want everything you've said,
And if you don't bring it now I'll eat you instead!'
So I rushed to the kitchen to find some white bread
But when I came back there were two monsters instead.
So I forced them down the stairs with a shiny little pin
But when they got down they went in the bread bin.

Donna Harrison (9)
St Luke's CE School, Warrington

Monster In My Drawers

There's a monster in my drawers
And has three chainsaws.
It creeps around at night
And gives everyone a fright
It flies like a bird
And everyone gets scared
It has sharp white teeth
And gives everyone grief
It watches me get dressed
And it makes me get stressed
It makes a bang
With a massive fang
I can't talk
But it can walk.

Daniel Horton (9)
St Luke's CE School, Warrington

The Dragon

There's a dragon in my room
My mum tries to whack him with a broom
It's going for my pet snake
When it's jumping on the bed it gives me an earthquake.

There's a dragon in my room
When it gets my homework I'm doomed
It's trying to make a fire
My mum, dad and sister are like a cats' choir.

There's a dragon in my room
It's heading to the church, it's attacking the groom
Oh no! it's coming back
It's chasing a duck and it's going quack!
Quack!

Julia Roberts (10)
St Luke's CE School, Warrington

Dragons

Dark dusty caves
This is what I hate
I always fear dragons
They will never be my mate.

Oh I can see one in my bed
He's wearing a body
His name is Ned
He's got a pole in his head
Why the worry?
I think he's dead.

Myles Duffy (9)
St Luke's CE School, Warrington

The Super League

Super League's great,
Super League's funny,
Saints and Leeds are just the best.
Unlike Wigan who are not that good.
Stevie O and Eddie are just mad
They make Super League great.
Harlequins and Huddersfield
Are in the top eight
Stevie O and Eddie are just great
Big Barry and Terry O'Connor are great.

Thomas Jones (9)
St Luke's CE School, Warrington

My Brother Is A Monkey

One day there was a bird called Larry
I bought him yesterday, he's eating all the food,
The goldfish too.
I wish he was in a zoo!
He's turned the place upside down,
His room is a mess but still he likes to live there.
He's eating all the food, he's turned this place into a zoo.
I will throw him out but he's my brother!
I want to throw my sister out too.

Elliott Harvey (9)
St Luke's CE School, Warrington

A Monster Poem

Beware, beware there's a monster in my bed
And there's a football post going through its head,
His eyes are blue, his teeth are red,
I don't think he's long been dead.
I stay up late every night,
Just to try to delay the fright,
The night is scary I'm beginning to dread
All because there's a monster in my bed.

Jack Baines (9)
St Luke's CE School, Warrington

There's A Carrot Under My Bed

There's a monster under my bed
It looks like a carrot
Please Mum, can I have some gravy?

There's a monster under my bed
It gives me the creeps in my body
And I don't know what to do.

There's a monster under my bed
I screamed in bed that night
And that was the end of him.

Caitlin Dutton (9)
St Luke's CE School, Warrington

Dragons

I found a dragon in my bed
He was bright, bright red.
His tail was very long
And he started to sing a song.
His ears were very floppy
And his hair was quite moppy.

Oh, if you're wondering it's a boy and a toy!

Chloe Murphy (9)
St Luke's CE School, Warrington

Teacher Trouble!

I was sat in the classroom
With my hand to keep me up.
But what tries to stop me?
The *teacher!*

My teacher tries to run around
After watching Everton win last night
We try to control him, 'Sit, stop, stay,'
But it's what we like to call
Teacher trouble!

After the maths lesson
It's time for break
But who tries to stop me?
The *teacher!*

My teacher tries to run around
After watching Everton win last night.
We try to control him, 'Sit, stop, stay,'
But it's what we like to call
Teacher trouble!

It's nearly the end of the day
He's just giving out homework
And I've got mine.
I try to escape
But who tries to stop me?
The *teacher!*

My teacher tries to run around
After watching Everton win last night.
We try to control him, 'Sit, stop, stay,'
But it's what we like to call
Teacher trouble!

Jessica Singleton (9)
St Luke's CE School, Warrington

The House Down The Road

The house down the road is a little scary,
An old woman lives there,
The house down the road is absolutely huge,
The old woman's a witch.

The house down the road is ghost-like,
The old woman's obsessed with housework,
The house down the road is as scary as our teacher,
The old woman's as crazy as Sam the student teacher.

The house down the road is dark and gloomy,
The old woman's off her rocker,
The house down the road encloses,
My mother!

Rachel Gaskell (9)
St Luke's CE School, Warrington

Friends

F is for fun
R is for responsible
I is for intelligent
E is for excellent
N is for noisy
D is for daring
S is for silly

Friends are forever
Fall outs are whatever.

Eleanor Bradford (9)
St Luke's CE School, Warrington

My Brother

D anger don't go near him, he's dangerous, he fights you
if you touch him
I dea, he always has got stupid ideas
S tinks, he stinks like a skunk but worse
A ngry when you mess with him he gets angry because he
always loses
S auce, he's got tomato sauce as his gunpowder
T errible, he's terrible when I'm trying to sleep,
he wakes everybody up
E vil, he's evil, very evil he's got potions in his attic
R ubbish, he's rubbish at everything, ask him a question
and he can't answer it.

Hollie Moore (10)
St Luke's CE School, Warrington

The Monster Poem

Beware, beware, there's a monster in my bed
If you look at him he will kill you.
He is dangerous, very dangerous, he will kill you in the house.

Beware, beware, there's a monster in my house
He will kill you and eat you, eat everything in the house,
And all the people in the house,
He is very scary, he has very long hair.

Josch Fairhurst (9)
St Luke's CE School, Warrington

What's That?

Is that a monster over the hill?
It's a monster over the hill
What's that next to it?
It's a dragon next to it
So many monsters, I can't count
They give me a fright.

Arran Heaton (9)
St Luke's CE School, Warrington

The Runescape Poem

Dharoks, Dragon, Granite and Rune
All these I'd love to have.
Oh Dharoks, Dragon, Granite and Rune
A shame I only have Oddy.

My mate has got full Rune and his name is Myles.
His armour is so good that he is jumping over stiles.

Jamie he has Oddy like me
But I have a rune weapon.
I'm not sure what ol' Jamie has
But I know it's not a bonespear.

Joshy J he has a Rune long
Not scimmy like mine nor singing a song.

Charlie Hewitt (10)
St Luke's CE School, Warrington

Witches

W itches waiting to cast a nasty spell
I n the bushes the witches are waiting
T he witches are wanting to kill us
C asting their spells onto them people
H ating them because they do not want a fight
E ating things to make them strong and win
S ick.

Bethany Shelmerdine (10)
St Raphael's RC Primary School, Stalybridge

The Time Of Macbeth

Macbeth longed to be king of Scotland
A man who fought in a ghastly battle every day
Crying for all of his lost teammates, who died a terrible death
Fighting for their country
Being a hero for Scotland's men and women
Everlasting war on the entire world
Three witches lurked in the shadows spying
on . . .
    Macbeth.

Liam Fullard (11)
St Raphael's RC Primary School, Stalybridge

War

War . . .
Fighting silence
Dying
Deadly silence
Gunshots . . .
Evil silence
Battlefield . . .
River of sadness
War is . . .waiting
Waiting is war . . .

Rhys Hadfield (10)
St Raphael's RC Primary School, Stalybridge

The Way Of The War

Witches covered by magic
Witches covered by mist,
Moans of the dying in the air,
Invading forces,
Death on the horizon,
The battle commencing.

The battle lingered
Witches watching,
Witches watching,
The armies torching houses
Despair was in the air.

Under the hills,
Celebrated the people,
No more chills of death,
Scotland prevailed.

Jack Fieldhouse (10)
St Raphael's RC Primary School, Stalybridge

Witches

Three witches awaited in a magical mist
Watching the Scottish kill,
They gloated, for people were in pain
The battle was really in vain.

Three witches awaited in a magical mist
Sniffing and testing the air,
It was nearly time for he who would come
He will nearly be there.

Three witches awaited in a magical mist
Watching the two remaining soldiers leave
One was Macbeth and the other Banquo
They went closer to see.

Michael Mansfield (10)
St Raphael's RC Primary School, Stalybridge

The Way The War Goes

The witches were watching, waiting,
Macbeth was fighting, attacking,
All the day, all the time, the witches waited,
While Macbeth was in war,
Macbeth was there.

Under the hills, the death of war,
Was waiting for Macbeth,
While still on the hills,
The witches watched, waited.

Then clatter, clatter, clatter,
Hooves, hooves, hooves,
The witches awaited their spell,
Macbeth was there.

James Shields (10)
St Raphael's RC Primary School, Stalybridge

Secret Spies

One day, some witches, they came
To watch people die in vain.
When the battle had died,
Some witches, they spied,
Over the battlefield for more people in pain.

On a horse, valiant Macbeth, he came,
Not one of the people in vain.
As he saw the magic makers,
He thought they were fakers,
And cried out, 'Soon we will meet again!'

Simon Kenworthy (10)
St Raphael's RC Primary School, Stalybridge

War Is A Dreadful Place To Be

War is a fight that never ends.
Fighting is guns and bombs.
Silence is a quiet place where you are . . .
Waiting for the war to end!

Dying is pain and death
Army is a ground that fights.
Victory is end.

Jack Forrest (10)
St Raphael's RC Primary School, Stalybridge

War Is Like . . .

War is like a fight that never ends.
Dying is like a pain or death.
Waiting . . .
For the war to
Stop.
Forces are as an army fighting for justice.
Gloating . . .
A prize possession . . .
Victory?

Chelsea Coop (10)
St Raphael's RC Primary School, Stalybridge

Waiting

W aiting, waiting for a fight
A fter the fight comes the dying
I t's the end of life
T ime has already ended for some
I n the end one side has one gone
N ever give up
G oing to the end.

Emma Cunningham (10)
St Raphael's RC Primary School, Stalybridge

The Three Witches

Trapped, trapped,
Defend.
High up, high up,
On the edge of the world.
Power, time's up.
Time's up, power.
Gone, gone,
Nobody's there.
Appearing, appearing,
Appeared.

Dying, dying,
Dead.
Watching, watching,
Gloating.
Invaders, invaders,
No longer there but trapped on the floor
Power raiser, power raiser,
More.
Victory, victory,
Over the invaders.
Gloating, gloating,
Dying souls.
Darker, darker,
The sun is black.
Fighting, fighting.
Finished.

Matthew Wardle (10)
St Raphael's RC Primary School, Stalybridge

The Triumph Of War

All day they watched,
The triumphant, horror of war.
The terrible trio of witches
Watched the mighty Scottish defeat
The invading army of Norway.
As the battle died and
The forces of Norway perished, the
Ghastly witches were gloating
Over the hundreds of the dead.

Joshua Ormerod (10)
St Raphael's RC Primary School, Stalybridge

War!

S un was covered by black clouds
H eaven was crying, watching the war commence
A man called Macbeth, sped from the battle
K ing Duncan's army fighting for king and country
E very man lying on the floor was gloated by three witches
S o even though the battle was won the hags knew a man had fled
P rotected an old feeble king this battle had done
E very daydream Macbeth dreamed, was him, ruler for all to see
A gainst the forces of Norway, the Scottish drove to victory.
R etreating from the battle Macbeth faced the driving rain
E ven though the battle was done the Scottish lost and won.

Robert Holding (11)
St Raphael's RC Primary School, Stalybridge

The Greatest Soldier

M acbeth the greatest soldier in King Duncan's army, for he was
A ll brave in every way, furiously angry to whoever messes with him.
C arefully dodging every obstacle of evil.
B oastfully destroying evil beasts from the horrendous pit of evil.
E very man would dream to be like him.
T all, clever and almost impossible to defeat.
H e is as brave as an ox.

Liam Manley (10)
St Raphael's RC Primary School, Stalybridge

The Sweet Light

Starlight will make you
Shine bright at night.

If you see this sweet light
Your dreams will always be alright.

The sun of the day
Lets us children out to play.

After the morning dawn
It keeps us nice and warm.

Hayley Sparks (9)
Whitby Heath Primary School

The Wind

A windy day is a blustery day
A blustery day is a windy day
Windy days I don't forget to wear my hairnet
Every hour the wind gets stronger
Every second the wind stays longer.

Cerys Holleron (8)
Whitby Heath Primary School

Healthy Living

An apple is juicy
A pear is soft.
We want to scoff
And eat the lot.

A cherry so sweet
That no one can beat.
An orange so bright
You can see it at night.

A banana so yellow
You'll scare the poor fellow.
The end of this rhyme is now near . . .
Don't ever drink *beer!*

Daniel Arathoon (9)
Whitby Heath Primary School

Doctor, Doctor

Oh doctor, doctor
I wish I could travel with you.

Every day, every night,
I wouldn't care if I got a fright.

All I want is to travel away with you,
Doctor, doctor . . .
Doctor Who?

Robyn Mercer (8)
Whitby Heath Primary School

Healthy

H ealthy makes you happy!
E at healthy food like
A pples - one a day
L ike fruit and vegetables too.
T omatoes are good but
H ot chips are bad for
Y ou.

Jordan Shrewsbury-Gee (9)
Whitby Heath Primary School

Me And My Piggy

Me and my piggy,
Going on our ride,
We find a farm
At the countryside.
We trotted down a hill,
Going past some trees,
As we went past them,
Out came some bees.
Because I was not looking,
I became close to a tree,
But so sadly,
Crash!

Emily Rigby (9)
Whitby Heath Primary School

Autumn Time

The trees are ready to fall asleep,
So watch the leaves come and
Dance at your feet.

Lots of colours they have been,
Yellow, green and in-between.

Oh what fun it has been to kick the
Leaves right up to my knees.

Now it's time to go back in and
Watch the leaves drift in the breeze.

Amy Hammond (7)
Whitby Heath Primary School

Dr Who

In the Tardis, off we go,
It goes very fast and very slow.
There's lots of crew
Doctor, Rose and Mickey too.
They save the world
All the time.
I really think
They're very kind.

Siobhan Franka (8)
Whitby Heath Primary School

Keeping Healthy

You should always try to keep healthy,
Your fitness will get high.
I'm running so fast, fast,
It almost feels like I can fly.
Drinking water, having plenty of sleep,
Five a day vegetables
To help you leap.
Do not eat sugar and do not eat fat.
We get unhealthy by eating that.
Having a shower and brushing our teeth,
By doing all this
We save ourselves grief.

Callum Hayes (9)
Whitby Heath Primary School

Friends

Friends can be made anywhere,
Even at school,
They can be made on the street,
Or made at home,
It doesn't matter, it's only if you
Know they will protect you,
It's not if they're popular or have the
Brain of a scientist,
It's if you trust them as being your friend,
That's most important,
In the end.

Hannah McMurray (9)
Whitby Heath Primary School

Summer Fun

Splashing and swimming under the sun
Having lots of summer fun.
Burgers and chips, fries and crisps,
Brings a tasty taste to your lips.
Summertime is almost over
As I wish upon a four-leaved clover.

Olivia Garland (8)
Whitby Heath Primary School

I Remember I Remember

I remember, I remember the place where I was born,
The weeping willow trees when I got up at dawn.
I remember, I remember the apples ripe and red,
And the twinkling stars when I went up to bed.
I remember, I remember what I used to do,
I used to sit under the sun and hear the cows go moo.

Lauren Spruce (9)
Whitby Heath Primary School

Winter

Snow is falling
Winter's calling,
Spring is on its way,
Streams and rivers will be frozen soon,
When we sit with the fire on in the living room,
When the cows go 'moo' because they're so frozen in the freezing fields.

Nevielle Hearfield (9)
Whitby Heath Primary School

Keeping Healthy

It's good to be healthy, so watch what you eat,
Lots of vegetables, fruit and meat.

You will be well, your body will be fit
If you get out and walk and not just sit.

5 a day keeps the doctor away
if you keep doing this, healthy you will stay.

Tyler (10)
Whitby Heath Primary School

Poem

The apples are red,
And I eat bread,
All keeping me healthy,
So I am wealthy.
The bananas are yellow,
They make me feel mellow.

Staying healthy is fun
So give it a go!

Jake Ranley (9)
Whitby Heath Primary School

Riding On My Bike

Riding on my bike,
Cycling down a hill,
Riding on my bike,
The wind goes through my hair,
Riding on my bike,
My peddles go up and down,
Riding on my bike,
I'm right in front of a tree,
Then I go *stop!*

Katie Gooding (9)
Whitby Heath Primary School

The Town

The town is really busy,
Like a swarm of buzzing bees
That are all confused and dizzy,
Trying hard to do trapeze.

Buses are always coming in,
Hardly ever going out.
The town is always busy,
Such a lot to shout about.

Morgan Basnett (9)
Whitby Heath Primary School

The Material's Poem

Rubber is very bendy,
Sometimes stretchy too.
Card has many colours,
My favourite one is blue.
Paper flips and is used
For many different things.
Gold glows on ladies' fingers
As a wedding ring.

Lauren Evans (7)
Whitby Heath Primary School

A Little Mouse!

I got a letter, well quite a few,
From a little mouse who loves to chew.
He chewed the corners and the top,
It was all smudged,
Like it had been mopped.
He wrote in little letters
'Dear Helen'
Then underneath that he drew a melon.
He sent more and more,
It just wouldn't stop!
Tens and hundreds, lots and lots.
But there's one thing that he forgot.
One line . . .
What was his name and how did he know mine?

Helen Lyth (10)
Whitby Heath Primary School

Cat In The Window

Cat in the window
What can you hear?
The chugging of the trains
Rain splashing down on the road
Trees swaying side to side
And the curtains swinging.

Cat in the window
What can you hear?
The wind blowing gently
Milk bottles clattering together
Cars in traffic
And children sucking on their lollipops.

Eleanor Wightman (8)
Whitby Heath Primary School

What Is . . . The Sun?

The sun is a ginger cat
Curled up in a ball
It is a golden watch
Floating through the clouds.

It is a diamond
Proposing to the Earth
It is a yellow submarine
On the surface of the clouds
The sun is a torch
Burning on an everlasting light.

Christopher Anderson (11)
Whitby Heath Primary School

Me!

I have blue eyes,
I like a surprise,
I have blonde hair,
And a pet bear,
I am the older child,
And I'm really wild,
I have this friend,
Who drives me round the bend,
I have a best mate,
She is great,
I like school,
It is cool,
I like cheerleading,
And a bit of reading,
I like shopping,
But I do the mopping.

Leah Woods (9)
Whitby Heath Primary School

School

S is for school the place where we're taught
C is for classroom the place for a thought
H is for holiday the summer is so great
O is for oversleep, I'm going to be late
O is for office, where the teachers chill out
L is for learning, the most important no doubt!

Emily McCubbing (9)
Whitby Heath Primary School

Things I Love To Do . . .

I love to dance and sing
High, low, fast and slow
Anytime, anywhere,
Even if someone's there.
I love to travel in Mum's car,
To get to gymnastics (as it is far)
Jump, leap and roll over
Cartwheel, handstands and flipover.

They are the things I love to do.

Jessica Swindells (7)
Whitby Heath Primary School

I Am Winter

I am Winter
Cold is like fingers of ice
Santa is like a big blanket made from his beard
Snow is like a big ball of cloud
Frozen lakes are big, shiny mirrors
I am frozen in the silver snow
I put the frozen gems onto the webs
I am Winter.

Alice Simons (10)
Wistaston Junior School

Winter

I pour the cold into the air
I spread the dew on the grass
I freeze the spider's web like Christmas decorations
I am the snowman in the garden
I put the frost into its place
I force the people to dress up warm
I mix the gloss in the snow.

Grace Newton (10)
Wistaston Junior School

I Am Autumn

I push the acorns off the trees
I chase the squirrels back into their hutches
I call the brown conkers out of their little protection
I make the leaves fall off their trees and turn brown
I sprinkle sleep powder on the tortoises.
    I am Autumn.

Liam Smyth (10)
Wistaston Junior School

I Am Winter

I am Winter
I am Jack Frost
Covering the land in a coat of lovely shiny white
I am the ice in the wind
The spider's web, is my wonderful piece of art.
The freezing air is my breath
I like to put icicles on the large green trees
The frozen lake is a white diamond
Snow is like a velvet blanket of white
I am Winter.

Louis Cain (10)
Wistaston Junior School

Winter Is Like . . .

Cold is like an ice-cube in my fridge
Snow is like icing sugar
Sprinkled down on my cake
Frostbite is like a blusher being frozen
I am Winter.

Kyle Nicholas (10)
Wistaston Junior School

I'm Spring

I raised the flowers high up to the midday sky.
The snow dried up like a puddle eager to escape the ground.
I bring life for lambs
So they can jump about like spring.
The sun is a deep orange frisbee
Swooning through the lit up sky.
I persuade the animals to pounce out of their beds.
I am Spring.

Felicity Martin (10)
Wistaston Junior School

Autumn

I shorten the days by spraying darkness
I turn leaves from green to brown
I make fruit ripe, plump and ready to eat
When I dash around the garden, crunching the leaves from tree
                                                                           to tree.

Jack Bohannan (10)
Wistaston Junior School

Winter

I love the snow
It's as white as the sky
When the clouds have covered the beaming blue sky.

I love the sound of the crashing sea
And the waves sounding like a shipwreck.

The wind is God whistling to me
Giving me a sign of Heaven.

I love looking out
Of my bedroom window,
At the huge, dark black cloud,
It's like a sign of danger.

I love snowballs,
They are white, fluffy marshmallows.

Jack Steele (10)
Wistaston Junior School

About Winter

Snow is like depositing sugar
On my nice hot cup of tea.
Frozen lakes are like really cold water.
Cold is a blowing wind and cold air.
Ice skating is like walking on frozen water
Without falling over.

Adam Elson (10)
Wistaston Junior School

I Am Winter

I make the sky chilling cold
Snow falls gracefully in the blue chilling skies
Icicles stand still like frozen people
The trees stand still with icy beards
I make days lovely with icy blue skies
I sprinkle the snow on the trees like icing sugar
The snow is bright as Santa Claus' beard
I spook autumn till it disappears into
The misty fog on the spooky hills
The Christmas snow appears with a bit of magic from the
                                            wintry world
I make *bigger* children throw snowballs at the little children
    I am Winter.

Alex Heaton (10)
Wistaston Junior School

Winter

Cold is like an ice-cube in a frozen freezer
Santa is like a magical man
Flying in the snow, falling sky
Snow is like powder sprinkling onto a soft puffy cake
A frozen lake is like a sheet of glass growing over water
Ice skating is like a deer sliding on a frozen lake
The snow-covered trees drop their every last leaf
Onto the white blanket of snow.
    This is what winter is like.

Joshua Banks (10)
Wistaston Junior School

I Am The Cold Winter

I, Winter, make avalanches move
In the cold winter I rebuild caves for the bears to sleep in.
I turn trees green and brown to white snow,
I make the water change into ice.
I put the snow on the ground.
I blow the cold air into the warm air.
I put the snow flat, so people can use it for skiing and snowboarding.
I lay icy cold snow on the bright green grass.
A snowball is a soft marshmallow
It's a white ball of mash.

Casey Ramsden (10)
Wistaston Junior School

Winter

Cold is like a huge quilt hugging the Earth.
Snow is like sprinkled icing sugar.
A frozen lake is like a huge sheet of glass.
Snowball is a big soft white marshmallow.
Snow is a white, soft bird floating through the cold air.
I am the cold winter.
I bring the frosty breeze to the Earth.

Konnor Edge (10)
Wistaston Junior School

I Am Summer

I am summer, I put the yellow into the sun
I even put the sparkle into the sun.
I hear the children jump into the sparkling blue sea.
I persuade adults to buy children ice creams.
I make the days longer.

Sam Hough (10)
Wistaston Junior School

I Am Summer

I see an enormous ball of flaming lava coming towards us.
I see a sweltering boiling sun shining on the deserted desert.
I see the day star cooling down and switching with the moon.
Summer is a burning fiery shining sun sparkling on the salty sea
water.
Summer is a sharp, spiky blistering sun shining on the people on
the beach.

Ruairidh Johnstone (10)
Wistaston Junior School

I Am The Seasons

Spring
I am Spring, I bring the Earth back to life.
The fields in spring are Heaven.
Spring is like a sheep, giving birth to a baby lamb.

Summer
I am Summer giving the Earth its colours.
The summer sun is an oven warming the Earth like a roast chicken.
On the beach in summer, there are people sunbathing like a beached whale.

Autumn
I am Autumn chasing the squirrels up trees
The leaves in autumn are turning gold and brown.
Autumn is like the whole world dying.

Winter
I am Winter making the Earth cold.
The fields in winter are a massive iced cake.
Winter is like a monster scaring the sun away.

Alexander Flude (10)
Wistaston Junior School

Captain Dag

Terrifying,
Evil and smelly
Looks like a huge balloon
Eyes like balls on his head
Nose like a cramped hole on the top of his mouth
His teeth are black and mouldy, *er!*
Captain Dag smells like a skunk
His armpits smell of rats' blood
Feet! Don't go there!
He feels like a rotten apple, slimy
His bad habits -
Picking his nose and
Spitting everywhere
He likes killing and whipping people
He is a terrifying threat.

Thomas Slaney (8)
Wistaston Junior School

Pirate Skull

Mean, evil and scary.
Looks like a big, fat football
With a belly like a bouncing ball.
Green nose,
As big as an apple.
Blue eyes like
Two big stinky bowls.
Teeth like silver foil smell
Terribly bad.
Pirate Skull woofs and pongs.
Armpits like pongy sick
Feet like two stinky old dumps.
Feet slimy and hairy.
Rotten teeth smell.
Lips wet horrible and slimy.
Loves killing.
A terrifyingly, ugly sight.

Molly Ramsden (9)
Wistaston Junior School

Pirate O'Neill

He is built like a pig, mean, cruel and evil,
He looks like an enormous fat pig (*urrgh*)
Red eyes like a fat strawberry,
Pink nose like a pig's nose,
Yellow teeth with lots of gaps in-between,
Smelly Pirate O'Neill smells foul,
His armpits absolutely stink like rotten tomato
Feet like an unflushed toilet,
Feels like a crooked house but squidgy,
Rotten nose-picking thief
Steals stuff like treasure,
Loves making people walk the plank,
Likes killing people,
A terrifying, ugly sight.

Selina O'Neill (9)
Wistaston Junior School

Pirate Eye-Patch

Mean, horrible, fat, nosy
Looks like a giant skyscraper
His eyes are cross-eyed
His nose looks like a witch's nose
His teeth are black and crooked
Pirate Eye-Patch stinks
His armpits smell like an unflushed toilet
His feet smell like poo
Pirate Eye-Patch feels like an old granny
A nose-pickin' thief
Loves killing people
A very horrid sight.

Oliver Slaney (8)
Wistaston Junior School

Pirate Bryce

Terrifyingly, small and fat
Looks like an evil, mean, cruel lady
Her eyes are like bright blue fireworks
Her nose is as green as sparkling grass
Her teeth are as yellow as the sun
Pirate Bryce smells underneath her armpits
She feels slimy like a snail's skin
She is a nose picking thief
Loves making people walk the plank
She would leave me dead.

Bryce Bennett (8)
Wistaston Junior School

Pirate Peter Brother

Tall
Eyes like a sea
Mean
Nose
As red as a tomato
Teeth like yellow chips
Smells like cow poo
He spits on people
He trumps in their faces
Kills people
He is
A hideous sight.

George Rowlands (8)
Wistaston Junior School

Pirate Blood Bounder

Terrifyingly tall with a thin belly
Looks like a giant boat
Red eyes like a big dragon
Big green nose which looks like snot
Black teeth like tarmac
He walks like he's broke his leg.

Blood Bounder smells
Like rotten poo
And pongs
Badly.
Armpits like a fly's bottom
Feels like a big tall rubber
Or
A snail which is slimy.
A rotten treasure seeker
Loves hitting and killing people
An awful threat.

James Hartshorn (8)
Wistaston Junior School

Pirate Jack

He picks his nose,
And is very fat,
He is
A very rude pirate.
His teeth are extremely black.
He eats his bogies
And he's a pig
And his eyes are flaming red
Pirate Jack is very smelly
He pongs,
Stinks like a cow
His nose is a rotten apple
And he likes to sneak up
On people and
Kill them
He makes them
Walk the plank.

Emma Hassall (8)
Wistaston Junior School

Pirate Black Beard

He is mean,
Horrible,
Fat and big
Mean, not cute
Blue eyes like pigs
Snotty nose like big green balls
Black teeth like big rotten pigs
Smells like an armpit all day long
Feels like my nan's foot
Doing things he should not do
He does what he does
Not nice.

Natasha Adams (8)
Wistaston Junior School

Captain Cutlass

Terrifyingly, big and bold,
Looks like a bear,
Has eyes like a hawk,
Has a nose like an orange,
And teeth like pointed rocks,
Captain Cutlass is the name,
Captain Cutlass smells like a rotten banana,
Armpits like a stinking swamp,
Feet like an unflushed toilet,
Rough and hard, scabby and decayed,
Setting his parrot, super strong,
Bad as a banana,
Likes gunpowder and gold,
He would leave you like a fragile egg, dropped on the rocks.

David Palmer (8)
Wistaston Junior School

Pirate Patchy

Smelly, evil and cruel,
Looks like a huge, fat ball,
One-eyed horrid man,
Big nose with snot running down his face (yuck),
Teeth like razors, some missing and mouldy,
Pirate Patchy smells vile,
His armpits pong,
Feet stink really bad,
He feels like a shrivelled up prune,
Rotten, spitting man,
A killing thief,
A treasure hunter,
He picks his nose
And flicks it!
Loves pulling people's brains out!
If you met him you'd soon be dead,
But I don't doubt he'd like to meet you!

Lucy Brierley (8)
Wistaston Junior School

Pirate Jack

Ugly and fat
Looks like a big rag
Red eyes like yesterday's dinner
Green nose like an overgrown cabbage
Teeth like dirty stones
Pirate Jack smells like rotten apples.

Oliver Parker (8)
Wistaston Junior School

Pirate Smelly

Terrifying, mean, smelly, bold
Looks like a pig
Looks like a fashion freak.
Eyes are like a monster's eye
His nose is fat
His teeth are mouldy
His feet are smelly
Like smoky bacon.
His armpits reek,
He pongs,
And smells like a pig
If I touch he would feel like a rusty tree
And if I dare touch his teeth
They would feel like a slimy slug.
He picks his nose and drinks swamp water
And he eats humans.
And
He eats his socks!
He steals jewellery!
He loves killing people!
He is a murderer
If I ever met him I would be frightened too.

Tia Redmond (8)
Wistaston Junior School

Pirate Rot

Very tall and scary
Looks like a fierce fox
His eyes are like red crystals
Has a nose which is long and pointy
Has black mouldy teeth
Pirate Rot has armpits that smell like an unflushed toilet
He feels like an old toothbrush
He eats with his mouth full, he spits, and he's a sea thief
Likes having sword fights
An ugly thing.

Rebecca Davies (8)
Wistaston Junior School

Anger

I am a herd of elephants charging into you
I am a crane knocking over your house
I am a door trapping your fingers
I am a crusher breaking your favourite toy
I am a dog ripping up your homework
I am a teacher telling you off
I am your worst enemy
I am Anger!

Bryony Chapman (10)
Wistaston Junior School

Excitement

I make people jump around,
I give you anything,
I decorate the Christmas tree,
I win competitions,
I give away my money,
I make all the party food,
I work at a theme park,
I am excitement!

Hannah Davies (11)
Wistaston Junior School

Jealousy

I am a green monster stampeding through school
I am a possession being thrown in a pool
I am a knife stabbing through a boy
I am the crusher that broke your favourite toy
I am the bully pushing the girl
I am the stealer of the precious pearl
I killed the model, 16 years old
I ripped the story I was never told.

Hannah Thompson (10)
Wistaston Junior School

Happiness

I give you presents like Santa
I give you chocolates and love
I dance all day
I laugh like a hyena
I give you family and friends
I give you an everlasting holiday
I am like a rose swaying in the breeze
My friend is laughter
I am Happiness.

Sam Spencer (10)
Wistaston Junior School

Happiness

I make people laugh, smile and cry in pain and agony
Of worlds of jokes,
I make the people jump with joy,
I make children shout all day, in a planet of wonderland paradise,
I am the PS2, the fun for you,
I give you sweets and chocolate that shine.

Callum Parker (10)
Wistaston Junior School

Happiness

I get you through rough times
I'm like one thousand heavenly angels, guarding you through the
night.
I am a world full of smiles
I give food to the hunger and drinks to the thirsty
I am a flower in bloom
I'm an everlasting holiday in the Canary Islands
I give you family and friends
I'm like the golden sun, setting peacefully over the sea
I am Happiness.

Sarah Oakley (10)
Wistaston Junior School

Sadness

I make people cry,
I cut people's legs,
I make people fall over,
And crack their heads,
I call people names,
I tell people off,
I break their bones
And rip their hair off,
I am Sadness.

Rhys Bennett (10)
Wistaston Junior School

Happiness

Happiness is like the shining sun beaming down its light on the
Glistening blue sea.
Happiness is playing with your friends, down the street on a nice
summer's day.
The moon winked at me through the dark clouds.
Happiness is the breeze, ruffling through my hair on the top of a cliff.
Happiness is like being able to go wherever you want and never die.

Tom Corbett (10)
Wistaston Junior School

Nervousness

I make a stinging shiver run up your spine,
I make your knees wobble from side to side
I make you tremble and you won't want to go on stage
I make you go bright red in front of an audience
I give you butterflies in your tummy
I am the feeling, Nervousness.

Charlotte Curry (10)
Wistaston Junior School

Anger

I am the thing people fear in themselves,
I am the thing that destroys happiness within others,
I make you hate, hurt and hurl,
I hate all lovers,
I attack happiness like a lion and its prey,
I like to make people cry,
Nothing can stop me hurting your feelings,
I make you rip up your homework,
I make you call people names,
I am Anger.

Harry Robinson (10)
Wistaston Junior School

Sadness

I kick you,
I make you cry,
I hurt your feelings,
I make you lie, like the class liar,
I break your bones,
I make you scream,
I make you get told off like you never have before,
I pull your hair,
I make you look silly in front of your friends,
I make you shout like you're speaking down a microphone,
I am Sadness!

Joanne Freake (10)
Wistaston Junior School

Anger

I am a lynx jumping on its prey
I am like a peregrine falcon diving at its enemy
I am like a wild fire, burning in your mind
I am like a stampeding rhino causing destruction everywhere it goes
For I am Anger.

Ellis Lawley (10)
Wistaston Junior School

Anger

Anger is an earthquake coming out of your mouth!
Anger is a lion roaring in your head,
Anger is a volcano erupting all over you,
Anger is like a tornado spinning you around,
A tree hits you in the tummy,
I cut people's knees and arms,
I bang people's heads together,
I am Anger!

James Burgess (11)
Wistaston Junior School

Worried

I am like an earthquake shaking you from all sides,
I am like a thunderstorm charging down your ear,
I am someone pinching you forever,
I am a devil poking you in your back,
I am a herd of bulls coming at you,
I am like hailstones only going in your way,
I am like a jellyfish sting running down your spine,
I am Worried.

Stephanie Walkington (10)
Wistaston Junior School

Happiness

I give love, chocolate and flowers,
I make the birds sing sweetly for hours,
I bring wishes to everyone,
I am the kettle that laughs when I'm turned on,
I make you a sweetie wonderland,
I am a pop star not a brass band,
I am the taste of an iced bun,
I am the sparkle in the sun.
    For I am Happiness.

Rebecca Jones (10)
Wistaston Junior School

Anger!

Anger is like a great, big, deep hole closing in on you
Anger is 1,000,000 stamping elephants in your head
Anger is as painful and as deadly as a cobra's bite
Anger is 1000 charging rhinos coming at you
Anger is like someone poking a stick at your brain
Anger is the worst thing ever.

Josh Golding (11)
Wistaston Junior School

Anger

My mind is made to destroy
I crush your favourite toy
I scream and shout
I knock you out
I flush you down the toilet
I'm as mean as a monster
My heart is as small as a grain of flour
I am Anger.

Lauren Reece (10)
Wistaston Junior School

Anger

I am the monster that trashes all your toys.
I am the hit, the kick, and the punch trying to take over you.
I am the dog barking and growling in your face.
I am a thousand rhinos charging at you.
I am a shark biting at your boat.
I am the Devil eating your mind.
I am the biggest balloon that suddenly pops.
I am an elephant that stamps on your head.
I am your homework torn up into little bits and pieces.
I pop the armbands in the deep end of the pool.
I am Anger.

Jenna Shephard (11)
Wistaston Junior School

Happiness

Happiness is like flowers bursting out of its buds.
Happiness is a bucketful of sunshine, shining from the blue sky.
Happiness is like a newborn baby coming into the world so big.
Happiness is a big smile upon a happy face.

Abbie Broadgate (11)
Wistaston Junior School

Happiness

Happiness is the sun shining on you,
Happiness is like watching dolphins swim freely,
The football smiled at me, as it flew into the top corner of the goal,
Happiness is like swimming in the clear, deep blue sea,
Happiness is like decorating the Christmas tree on Christmas Eve,
Happiness is a bird tweeting peacefully in the morning sun,
Happiness is like one million stars, whispering your name in the
midnight sky.

Alexander Fitton (10)
Wistaston Junior School

Happiness

I am like a dazzling star made from millions of silver diamonds
I am a shining crystal ball predicting a fabulous future
I am a delicate dolphin jumping in and out of the wrinkly waves
I am a daring skier amusingly whizzing down slippery slopes
I am a beautiful butterfly, flapping its amazing wings
I am like a golden ball filled with irresistible exciting times.
I am Happiness.

Alice Woodbridge (10)
Wistaston Junior School

Anger

I am like a thousand rhinos coming out your mouth,
I am what makes you hit your friends when you are sad,
I am a red devil whipping you with my leathery tail,
I am a desert, crawling with dangerous spiders,
I am like a roaring fire, burning down your house,
I stare at you until you are red with fear,
I like to break your skis when you're winning a race,
I am like a red balloon full of fire,
I make your knees wobble and shake,
I cut your skin when you peel potatoes,
I am Anger.

Alan Hoodless (11)
Wistaston Junior School